Richard Meier
Smith House
Douglas House

Residential Masterpieces 17
Richard Meier
Smith House
Douglas House

Text and Edited by Yoshio Futagawa
Photographed by Yukio Futagawa
Art direction: Gan Hosoya

Copyright © 2014 A.D.A. EDITA Tokyo Co., Ltd.
3-12-14 Sendagaya, Shibuya-ku, Tokyo 151-0051, Japan
All rights reserved. No part of this publication may be reproduced,
stored in a retrieval system, or transmitted,
in any form or by any means, electronic, mechanical,
photocopying, recording, or otherwise,
without permission in writing from the publisher.

Copyright of photographs
©2014 GA photographers

Printed and bound in Japan

ISBN 978-4-87140-642-0 C1352

Residential Masterpieces 17

Richard Meier

Smith House

Darien, Connecticut, U.S.A., 1965-67

Douglas House

Harbor Springs, Michigan, U.S.A., 1971-73

Text by Yoshio Futagawa

Photographed by Yukio Futagawa

世界現代住宅全集17
リチャード・マイヤー
スミス邸　1965-67
アメリカ合衆国，コネチカット州，デリエン

ダグラス邸　1971-73
アメリカ合衆国，ミシガン州，ハーバー・スプリングス

文・編集：二川由夫

企画・撮影：二川幸夫

GA

スミス邸，ダグラス邸－モダニズムを継ぐもの──二川由夫
Smith House, Douglas House — In the Footsteps of Modernism *by Yoshio Futagawa*

リチャード・マイヤーの初期の住宅である「スミス邸」(1965-67年)と「ダグラス邸」(1971-73年)は，彼の長いキャリアの中，単に初期の名作であるというだけでなく，そのクオリティの高さは現在でもまったく色あせることなく，モダニズム建築のハイライトとして再び訪れるに値する名作住宅である。「スミス邸」，「ダグラス邸」ともに40年以上の歳月を経ても，竣工当時と変わらない輝きが保たれている理由は，住み手の建築に対する愛情の深さに他ならない。「スミス邸」はオリジナルオーナーの息子が受け継ぎ，完璧な姿を維持し続け，「ダグラス邸」は数世代のオーナーの交代，改築を経て，現在はオーナーの努力によって竣工時の状態に戻されている。2軒の住宅は時を超えて生きている。

1960年代後半より，建築家としての本格的なキャリアをスタートさせたリチャード・マイヤーは，J・ヘイダック，C・グワスミー，P・アイゼンマン，M・グレイヴスらとともに「ニューヨーク・ファイブ」と呼ばれた。彼ら共通の主題は，ル・コルビュジエをはじめとする近代建築の先人たちが構築した建築理論の継承・展開であったが，それらは戦後の現代建築に，アメリカ人好みの明快でクリアな方法論としてのモダニズム＝より「ゲーム化」された建築の組み立て方をもたらした。

マイヤーはこの5人の中にあって，これまでのキャリアの中でもっとも一貫した姿勢をとり続けている建築家である。初期の住宅作品から「ゲティ・センター」(1984-97年)などの大規模な建築まで，コルビュジエの建築理論に忠実で，フォロワーとしてその先にあるべき発展形を実現して見せてきた。彼はキュービズム的な平面構成──フリープランの手法，平・立面のモデュールとなるグリッド上に展開される要素の均整を追求し，端正で分析的な空間構成を探求する。それらは一元的な完結性にとどまらず，さらにコルビュジエの提唱した建築システムすらコラージュすることで，新しく多元的に完結したモダニズムの結晶をつくりだした。コルビュジエの建築システムは，ここで建設のタイポロジーの側面をそぎ落とされて純粋な建築言語に昇華している。

「スミス邸」と「ダグラス邸」は兄弟住宅である。「ダグラス邸」のオーナーは最初，「スミス邸」の図面を買いたいとマイヤーの所に来たことから設計が始まった。しかし，外装が白いということだけで，その案は敷地のある地域の建築審査に通ることができず，新しい敷地を買い，新しい案の住宅を建てることになった。敷地の状態は違うが，要求されたプログラムが近似的であり，内部の基本的な空間構成は似ている。寝室などを収める閉じたプライベート・スペースと，周囲の風景に開かれた居間・食堂などのパブリック・スペースの二元的な構

Smith House (1965-67) and Douglas House (1971-73) are not only Richard Meier's early masterpieces in his long career but outstanding houses of never-fading quality that are worth revisiting as highlights of Modernist architecture. What makes both houses continue to retain their original luster after more than 40 years since completion is nothing other than the residents' deep passion for architecture. Smith House, passed on to the original owner's son, perfectly maintains its appearance to this day, while Douglas House, through a series of change of ownership and renovations over time, is now brought back to its former glory through efforts by the present owner. The two houses are alive, transcending time.

Richard Meier started his career as a full-fledged architect in the late 1960s and was among The New York Five with J. Hejduk, Ch. Gwathmey, P. Eisenman and M. Graves, who shared a common theme of succession and development of architectural theories crafted by the predecessors of modern architecture such as Le Corbusier, that have introduced Modernism to the post-war contemporary architecture, as a clear-cut methodology to the Americans' liking—a more 'game-like' way of architectural composition.

Meier has been the most consistent among the five in terms of attitude through one's architectural career. From his early series of residential works to large-scale architecture such as the Getty Center (1984-97), he realized what he believed would be the advanced form of Le Corbusier's architectural theories as a faithful follower. His pursuit of Cubist plane composition—the free-plan method and balance of elements deployed over the grid as plan/elevation modules—lead him to explore spatial compositions that are orderly and analytic, that go beyond a one-dimensional completeness, creating Modernist crystals with multidimensional completeness by organizing architectural systems proposed by Le Corbusier in collages. There, the typological side of construction is trimmed away from Le Corbusier's architectural systems in order to sublimate them to pure architectural language.

Smith House and Douglas House are house siblings. The owner of Douglas House initially visited Meier in hope of purchasing the plan for the Smith House. Meier began designing the new house but his plan was rejected by the local building review council for the sole reason that its exterior was white. Eventually, another location was purchased to build a house with another plan. Although the condition of the site is different, the requested programs are approximate and the basic interior space makeup is similar. Its dual composition, consisting of enclosed private spaces accommodating the bedrooms and public spaces such as the living and dining rooms that open toward the surrounding landscape, features a distinctive characterization in terms of elevation as 'layers' and 'open ceiling spaces.' They are accomplished using Le Corbusier's ar-

成，それは断面においても「層」と「吹き抜け」として明快に性格分けがなされている。これらはコルビュジエのシトロアンとドミノの建築システムによって達成され，二つの性格の異なる建築システムがここで一つにコラージュされている。

アメリカの建築は，イギリスの植民地時代より基本的にヨーロッパから輸入された様式の発展形である。アメリカに元々あった様々な条件に対して，ローカライズされていった独特の建築文化が根底にある。例えば，トーマス・ジェファーソン設計の「ヴァージニア大学」のLawnと呼ばれる伽藍や，自邸である「モンティッチェロ」で用いられたローマやパラディオなどの歴史様式の引用は，そのスケールやプランニングなど，独自な与件によって，ローカライズ＝アメリカナイズがなされている。これは建設技術や，それに拍車をかけるように，工法（石造，煉瓦造vs木造）の違いによるオリジナルとの違いも大きい。アメリカは現在，概して大スケール空間の国であると認識されがちだが，その創生期にはつつましいピューリタンの精神に始まるコロニアル・スケールの建築が多く見られた。スケールダウンされた空間に無骨化された装飾のオーダーが与えられ，アメリカ的な建築がつくられる。植民地的な気楽さを纏い，漫画の様に単純化・合理化され，解り

やすい建築，それがアメリカの民主主義社会を収める建築の基本であった。

「スミス邸」と「ダグラス邸」を改めて訪れると，当時のマイヤーの建築理念が木造によって見事に結晶化されていることに驚かされる。コルビュジエの理念は従来の石や煉瓦による組積造から脱却し，コンクリートや鉄といった当時の新素材による建設が前提に純化されていた。ピロティがスラブと柱という二つのエレメントだけで成立できるのは，その材料のソリッドな非物質的な特性に負っている（「サヴォア邸」などの戦前，白の時代の住宅は，実際にはコンクリート構造にブロック壁が充填され，それらが区別無く白く塗り込められているものも多い）。しかし，マイヤーが，美しい平面図やアクソノメトリック・ドローイングによって明示される，建築的に見事に解かれているロジックを，実際には木造によって表現していることは興味深い。「スミス邸」の工事現場の写真を見ると，鉄製の丸柱が見られるものの，木造によって建設が進められている様がよく解る。ガラスの大窓は木造の枠によって収められている。しかし，白ペンキによってすべてが均質に塗り込められて木造の建物が非物質化を意図されようとも，木の記憶はそこに留まり，空間に与えている効果は大きい。

それは，ヨーロッパ発のモダニズム建築がここでローカライズされ，

chitectural systems Citrohan and Dom-Ino: here, two architectural systems with different characters are put together in a collage.

Since the times of British colonial rule, American architecture has basically been a progressed form of imported European architecture. It is rooted in a unique architectural culture of localization in response to diverse conditions indigenous to America. For instance, historical references such as Rome and Palladio found in The Lawn in Thomas Jefferson's University of Virginia or his home Monticello are localized = Americanized in terms of scale and planning according to unique given conditions, where difference in construction technology and building method (masonry, brick construction vs. wood construction) from the original played a greater part. America today tends to be acknowledged as a country of large-scale spaces, but at the stage of the nation's creation, many of its architectures were in Colonial scale born out of the frugality of Puritan spirit. American architecture consisted of small-scale spaces with rustic decorative orders. The basics of architecture that accommodated the American democratic society were cartoon-like, simplified, streamlined, straightforward architectures with an easy, Colonial air.

Upon a renewed visit to the two houses one is amazed at the spectacular crystallization of Meier's architectural principles of the time in the form of wooden structure. Le Corbusier's principles were refined by breaking away from the conventional masonry construction of bricks and stones and on the premise of construction using concrete and steel that were new materials back then. A piloti to stand with only two elements, slab and column, depends largely on the materials' solid, non-physical attributes (many houses from the pre-war 'era of white' such as Villa Savoye are concrete structures filled with block walls all painted uniformly white). However, what is intriguing is the fact that Meier opted for wood structure to express the logic, a superb architectural solution, that is clearly indicated in his beautiful floor plans and axonometric drawings. Photographs of the construction site of the Smith House shows the wooden structure of the building, with the exception of some steel pillars. But everything is painted uniformly white: despite the intention for a non-physical wooden structure, the memory of wood lingers while having a considerable effect on the space.

In other words, the European-born Modernist architecture was localized here and emerged as an 'American-style residential architecture.' This appearance plays a major role in giving these two buildings their vernacular character as well as warmth and feelings that are essential to a house. While the vertical wood panels on the wall are all painted white, the rich wooden texture still shows—it is firmly connected to the flavor that the typical American residential architecture has nur-

「アメリカ風の住宅建築」として現れているということである。この現れ方が，これら二つの建築にヴァナキュラーな性格や，住宅に必要な暖かみや情感を大いに与える役目を果たしている。堅羽目の木の壁面は白ペンキによって塗りつぶされていても，そのテクスチャーは木造の豊かな質感をたたえ，それはアメリカの典型的な住宅建築が育んできた風情に確実に繋がっている，ノスタルジーすら醸し出すものである。たとえば，チャールズ・ムーア／MLTWの名作，「シーランチ・コンドミニアム」の内部において，大胆な色彩の「スーパー・グラフィック」に塗り分けられて飾られていても，そこには背後の木造の暖かみが強く感じられ，カリフォルニアの典型的な木造建築と確かに接続していることを認識するのと同様，マイヤーの住宅が異端の白い現代建築ではなく，「アメリカの住まい」の系譜に確実に属していることが解る。

さらに，内部における様々なディテールを観察すると，それらは親しみのある人間的な良い意味での「無骨さ」がある——それは厚みであったり，ハンドレールや開口部の寸法，ディテールであったり，白く塗りつぶされた煉瓦造の暖炉であったり，そして後年，マイヤーのトレードマークになっていく大胆なピアノ・カーブであったりする。繊細さを主張するのではなく，解りやすく大振りなアクションを伴って主張するアメリカ的な要素を発見することができる。

歴史様式を引用するポストモダニズム建築が，合理的で無機質な近代建築に取って代わり，アメリカ中でポピュラリティを獲得するのはこれらの住宅が建ってから10年ほど後のことになるが，このムーブメントがアメリカで市民権を獲得した理由の一つは，参照した建築言語の解りやすい見せ方であった。引用する建築理論や言語のコントラストを取り上げ，ゲーム化された知的操作によって戯画化（＝ポップ化）することで，歴史様式はアメリカ的な解りやすさや親しみが与えられ，その上，重厚なヨーロッパの歴史との接続による満足感を新大陸が獲得するという，大衆化の手立になった。

マイヤーの建築は単なるモダニズム継承と発展ではなく，それを読み替えて重層的にコラージュし，批評性を与えることであり，そこに生まれた建築，言語は，戦前に建てられた一連のコルビュジエの白い家が本来持つ，ソリッドでシャープな造形とは異なり，アメリカ独自の文化に対応する形でローカライズされた，それは文字通りの「ポスト・モダン建築」であったと言えよう。アメリカの建築の特質を見るようでたいへん興味深い。

アメリカナイズされたモダニズムとしてのマイヤーの建築は，「スミ

tured, and even radiates a feel of nostalgia. For example, in the Sea Ranch Condominium, Charles Moore/MLTW's masterpiece whose interior is decorated with Supergraphics with bold, distinctive colors, one can clearly feel the warmth of wooden structure in the background and recognize an evident connection with the typical Californian wooden architecture. In a similar way, Meier's houses, rather than being unorthodox white contemporary architectures, belong to the lineage of the 'American dwelling' with absolute certainty.

Further examination of various interior details reveals their 'rustiness' in a good sense, friendly and human, that is demonstrated in thicknesses, size and details of handrails and openings, the brick fireplace painted in white, and the bold piano curve that eventually became Meier's signature design in later years. There can be found elements that are typically American, speaking out with straightforward, dramatic actions rather than subtlety.

Although it will take 10 years after the completion of these houses for the Postmodernist architecture that borrows references from historical styles to take over from the rational, inorganic modern architecture and gain popularity across America, one of the reasons this movement became widely accepted in America was the straightforward display of the referenced architectural language. By picking up the contrast of referenced architectural theory and language and caricaturing (= popularizing) it through game-like intelligent manipulation, American straightforwardness and friendliness were given to historical styles, as they became a means of popularization when the New World achieved a feeling of satisfaction through its connection to the dignified European history.

Instead of simply focusing on continuation and development of Modernism, Meier's architecture involves finding new ways of reading it, assembling elements in multi-layered collages and adding a critical character to it. The resulting architecture and language are, unlike the series of white houses built by Le Corbusier before the war and their solid, sharp figures, 'Postmodernist architectures' in literal terms, localized to suit a culture unique to America that prove to be quite interesting as demonstrations of the very nature of American architecture.

Meier's architecture as an Americanized version of Modernism, with its nostalgic atmosphere of typically American residential architecture found in his early residential works such as the Smith House and the Douglas House, will eventually make it possible to export globally, as its American type of systematic rationality = building method transformed into an exterior system consisting of panels that account for his unique, orderly joint layout.

ス邸」と「ダグラス邸」などの初期の住宅に醸し出されるアメリカ独自の住宅建築に漂うノスタルジックな香りから，アメリカ的なシステマティックな合理性＝工法においては独自の端正な目地割をもたらすパネルによる外装システムへと変貌して，世界的な流通を可能にしていくことになる。

「スミス邸」と「ダグラス邸」をはじめとする住宅の仕事以降，マイヤーは合衆国のみならず世界中に様々なビルディング・タイプのプロジェクトを手がけ，今日，世界的な建築家として認知されている。彼の手がけてきたあらゆる建築は，常に初期の住宅作品同様に，明快なロジックとアナロジー，繊細で密度の高いデザインによって生み出されていて，そのアウトプットには明確な建築家の署名が与えられている。半世紀にわたり変わりゆく時代の要請に適応しつつ，自身のスタイルを崩すことなく，ポピュラリティを獲得している数少ない現代建築家である。

現代の多くの建築家にとって小規模の住宅設計がそのキャリアの原点となることは珍しくないが，次第にスケールの大きな公共性のある建築に仕事を移していっても，初心に立ち返るがごとく住宅設計を手がけることは建築家の本心と実力の真価を検証し，世に表明するものである。大スケールの建築ではなかなか気がつかないディテールやプロポーションの微差がもたらす，空間への豊かな日常効果を住宅設計によって検証することの有効性は，近代建築の巨匠＝ル・コルビュジエやフランク・ロイド・ライトが生涯にわたって手がけた住宅群を見れば明白である。

「スミス邸」と「ダグラス邸」はマイヤーの出発点であり，今や世界中に実現されているマイヤー作品の系譜に通底するデザイン手法のエッセンスと建築へのスピリットが，純粋で瑞々しく内包されている名作住宅である。そしてマイヤーは近代の巨匠たち同様，今日でも住宅を手がけ続けている。住宅からハイライズや美術館などの大建築まで，規模や時代を横断してマイヤーの建築は探求され続けていると同時に，その思想と手法は「スミス邸」と「ダグラス邸」という最初期の作品においてすでに完成されていた。2軒の住宅は今も輝き続けている。

Following his residential works including the Smith and Douglas Houses, Meier has been involved in projects for various building types inside and outside the US, and came to be recognized as a worldwide architect today. All of his architectures are, as it was the case with his early residential works, always created out of clear-cut logic and analogy and his design of subtlety and rich density, and his output bears the architect's distinctive signature. He is one of the few contemporary architects who managed to gain popularity without having to alter his own style over the last half century as he continues to adapt to the needs of the times.

For many architects today it is not uncommon that small-scale residential design becomes the starting point of one's career, but even as the focus gradually shifts toward public projects of larger scales, working on residential design, like an act of going back to the basics, is an opportunity to put to test the architect's true mindset and ability and present them to the world. The effectivity of reviewing through residential design the rich, day-to-day spatial effects brought by minute differences in details and proportions that are hard to notice in large-scale architecture, is incontestable as one looks at the series of residential works that the masters of modern architecture such as Le Corbusier or Frank Lloyd Wright had created over the course of their lives.

Smith House and Douglas House represent Meier's starting point: they are residential masterpieces that encompass his architectural spirit and essence of design method that underlie the lineage of Meier's works realized all over the world today, fresh and pure. And Meier, like modern masters, continues to create houses to this day. From houses to large architectures such as high-rises and museums, Meier's quest in architecture keeps straddling different scales and time periods, while his ideas and methods had already been perfected in the earliest of his works, Smith House and Douglas House. Today, the two houses still continue to shine.

English translation by Lisa Tani

Smith House 1965-67

Overall view from east

Site plan

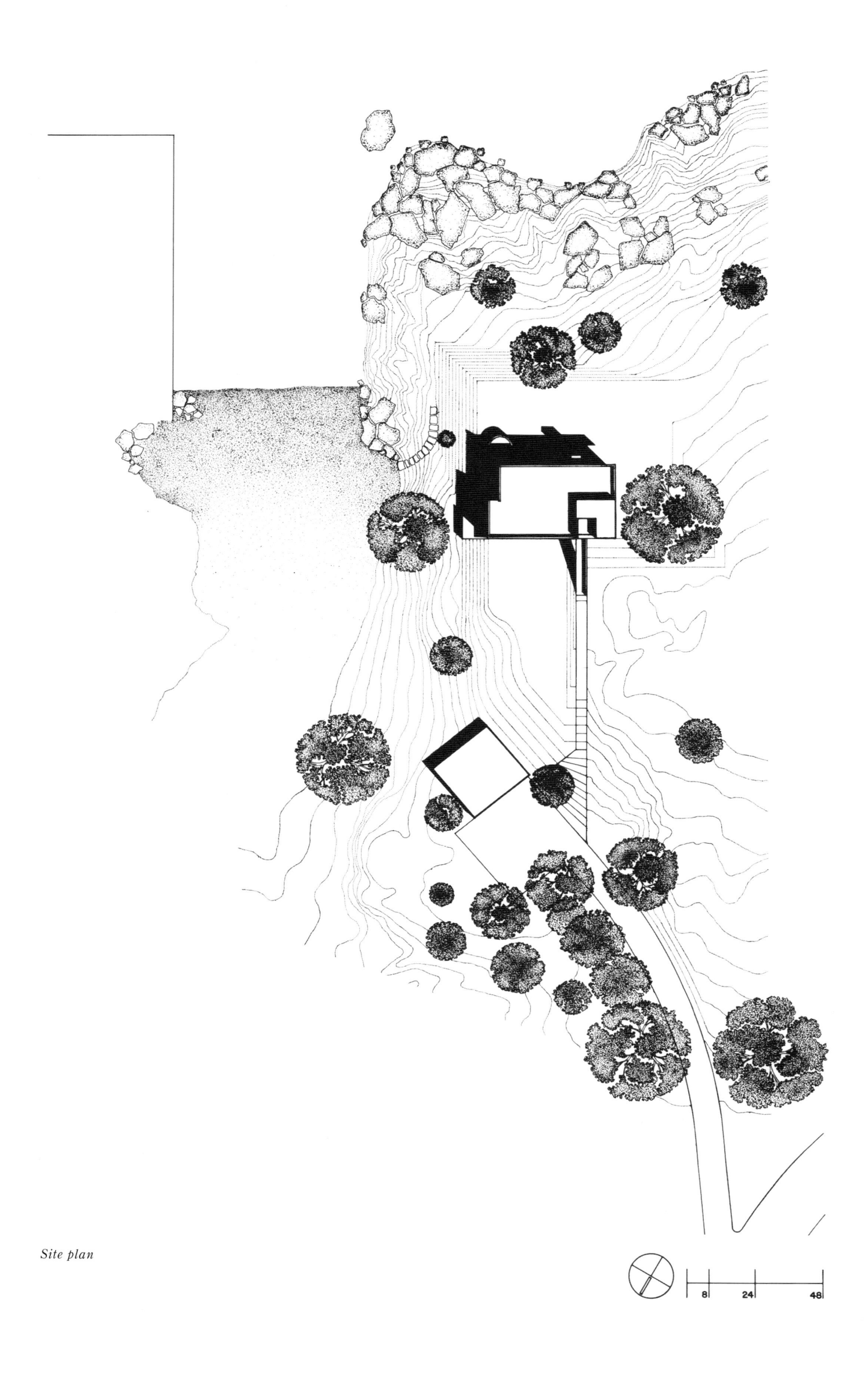

View from east

View from south

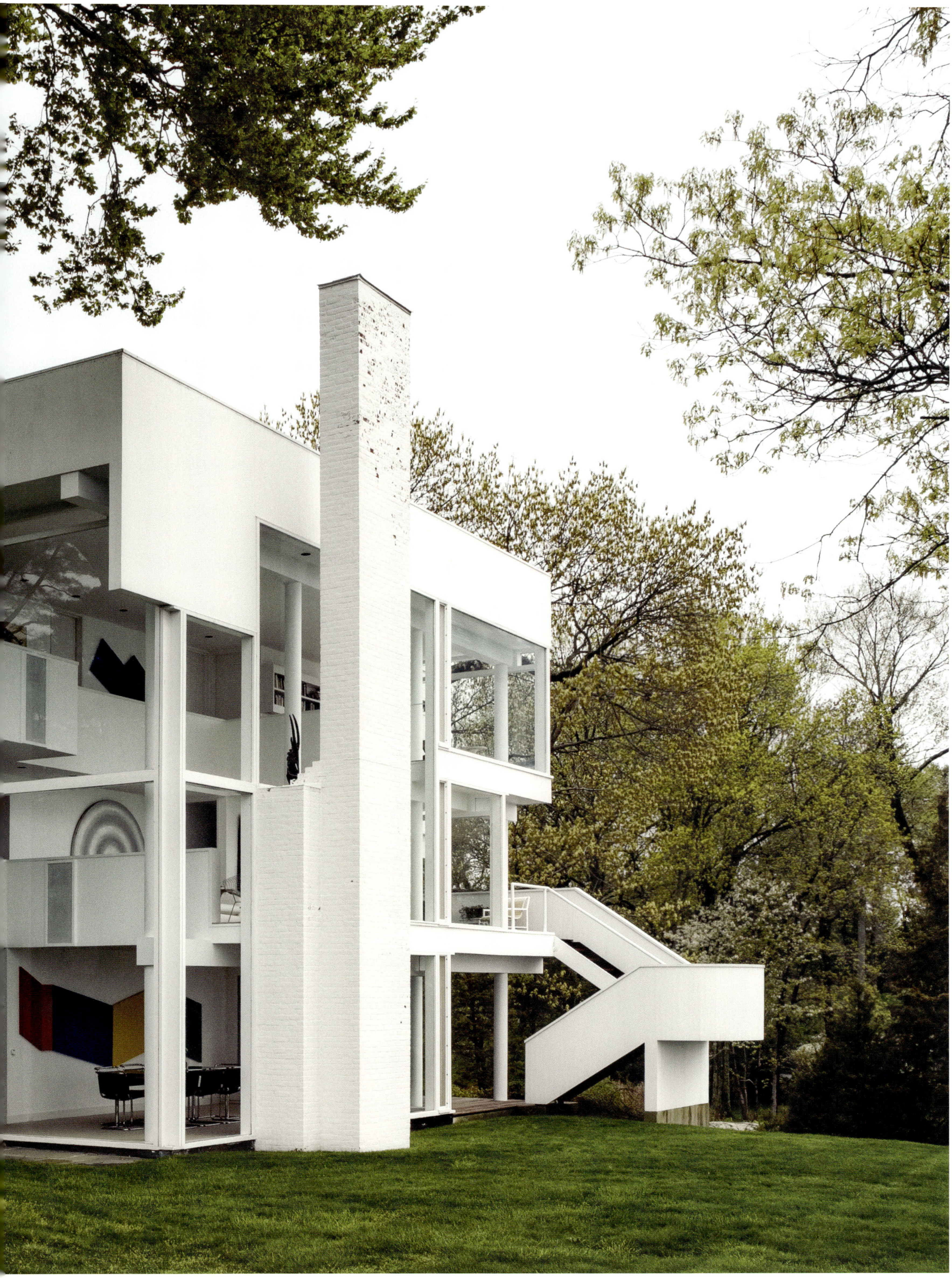

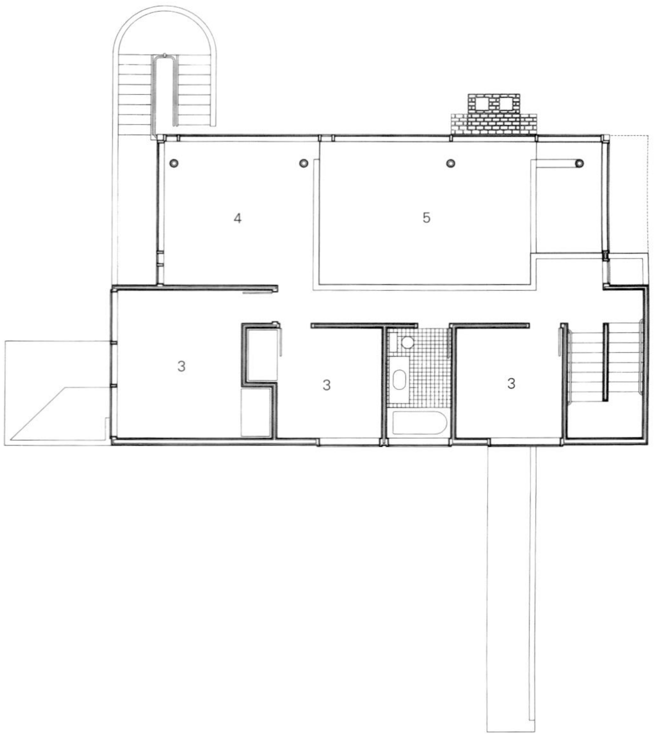

Upper level

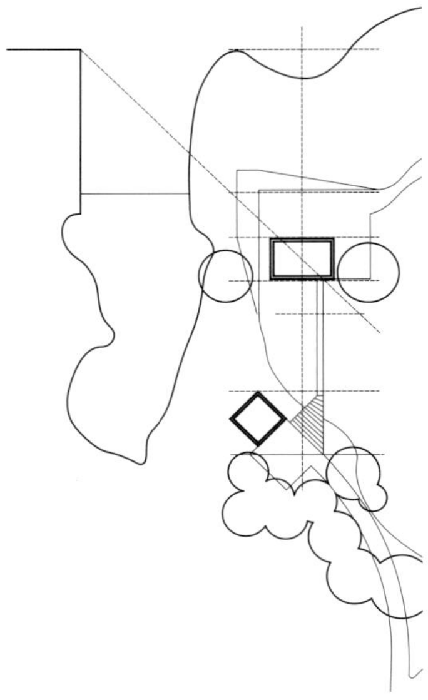

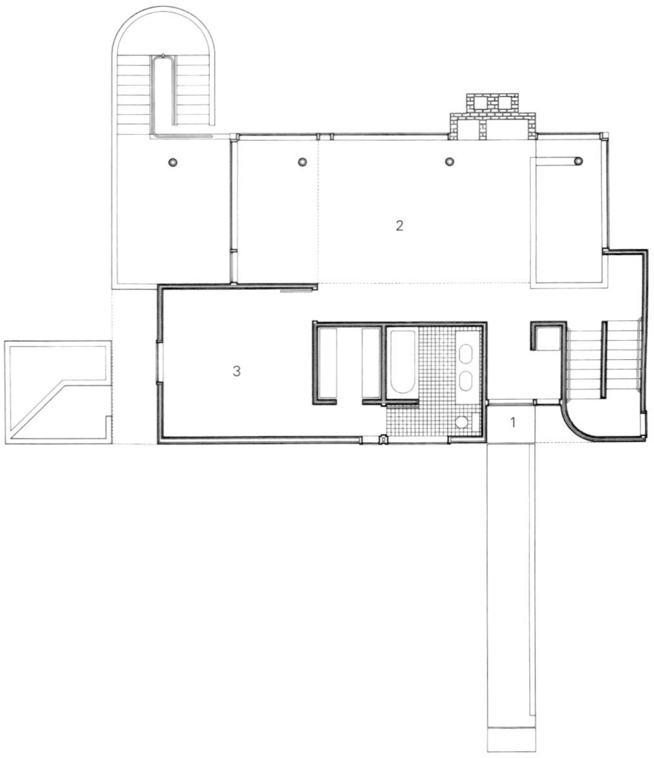

Middle level

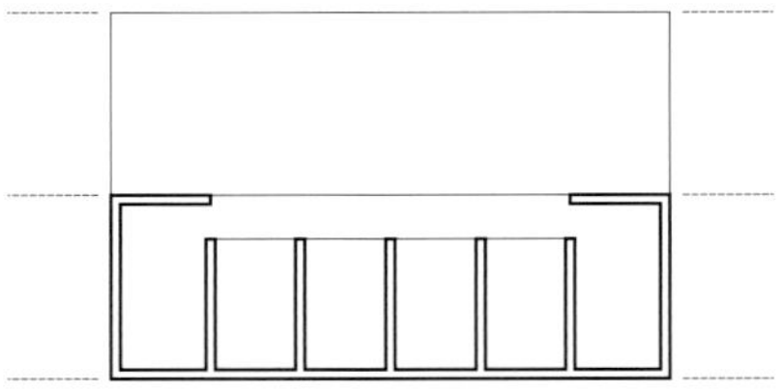

Lower level

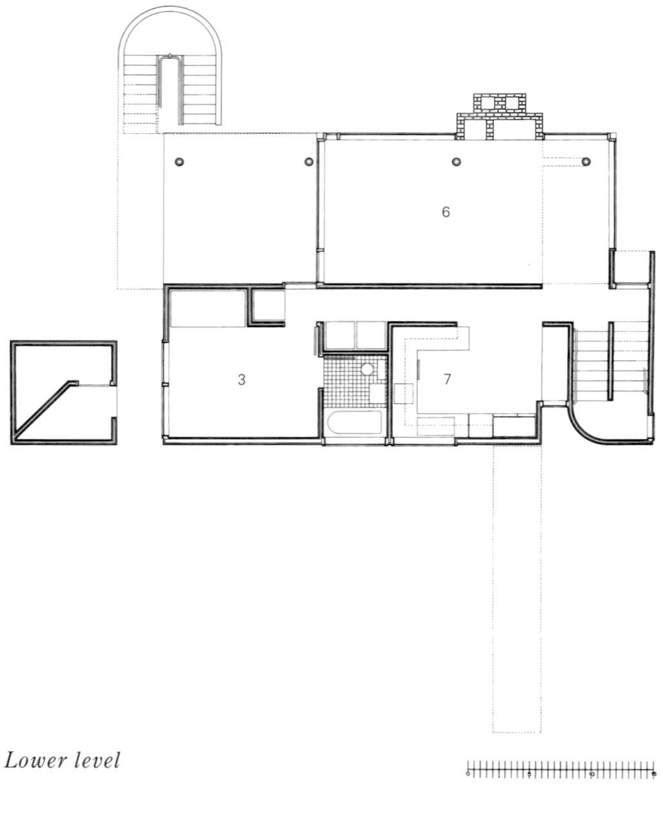

1 ENTRANCE
2 LIVING ROOM
3 BEDROOM
4 STUDY
5 VOID
6 DINING ROOM
7 KITCHEN

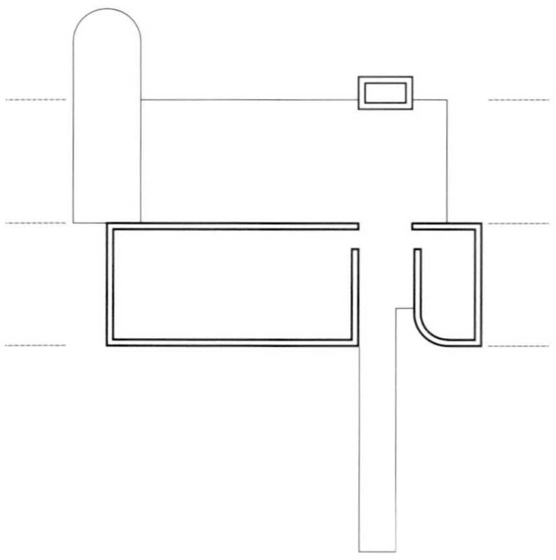

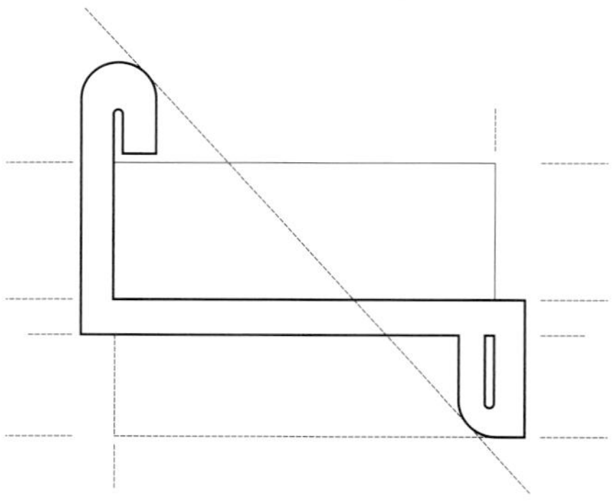

Site

Program

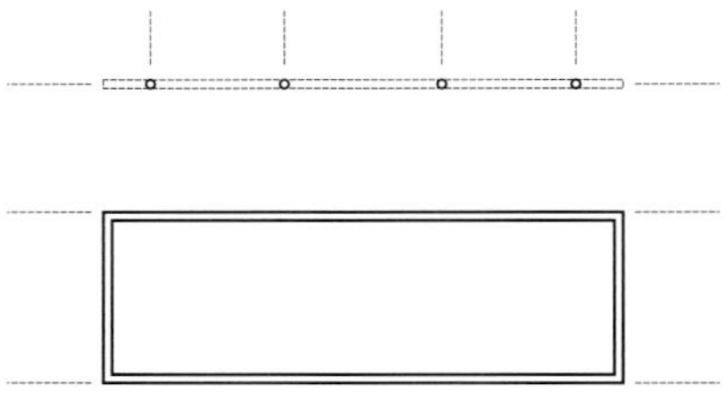

Structure

Entrance

Circulation

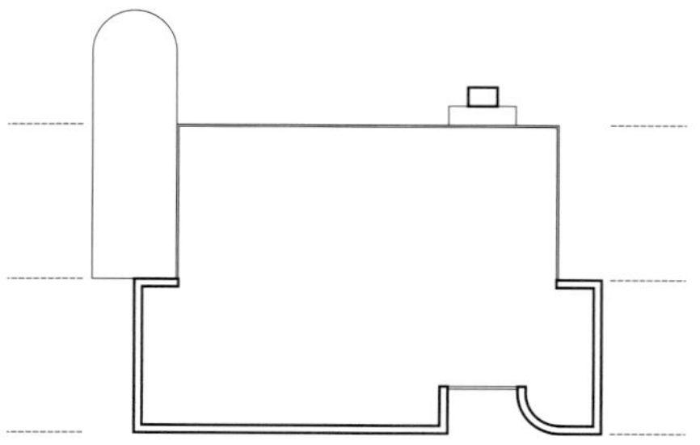

Enclosure

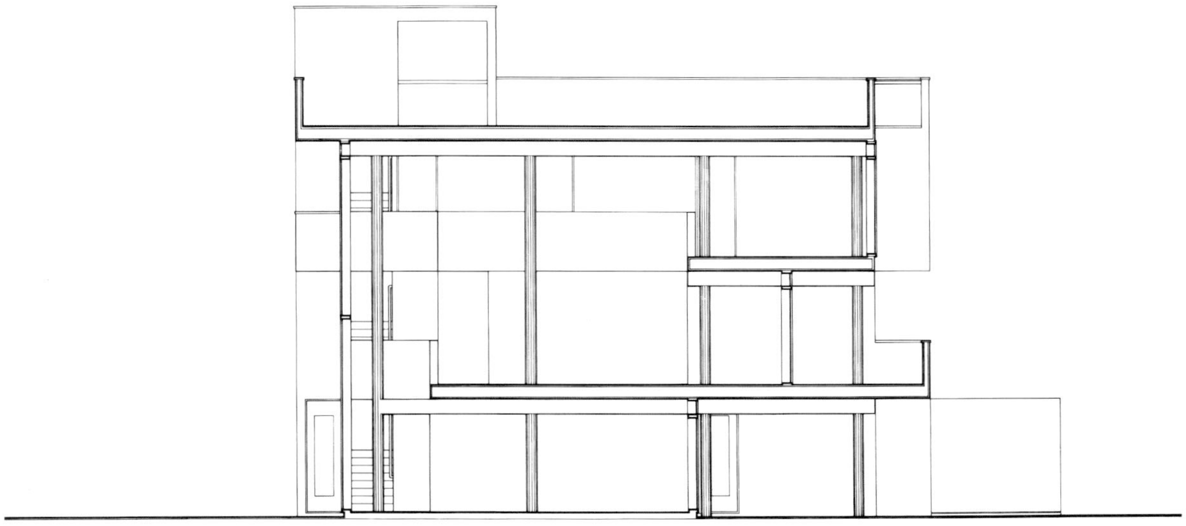

Longitudinal section

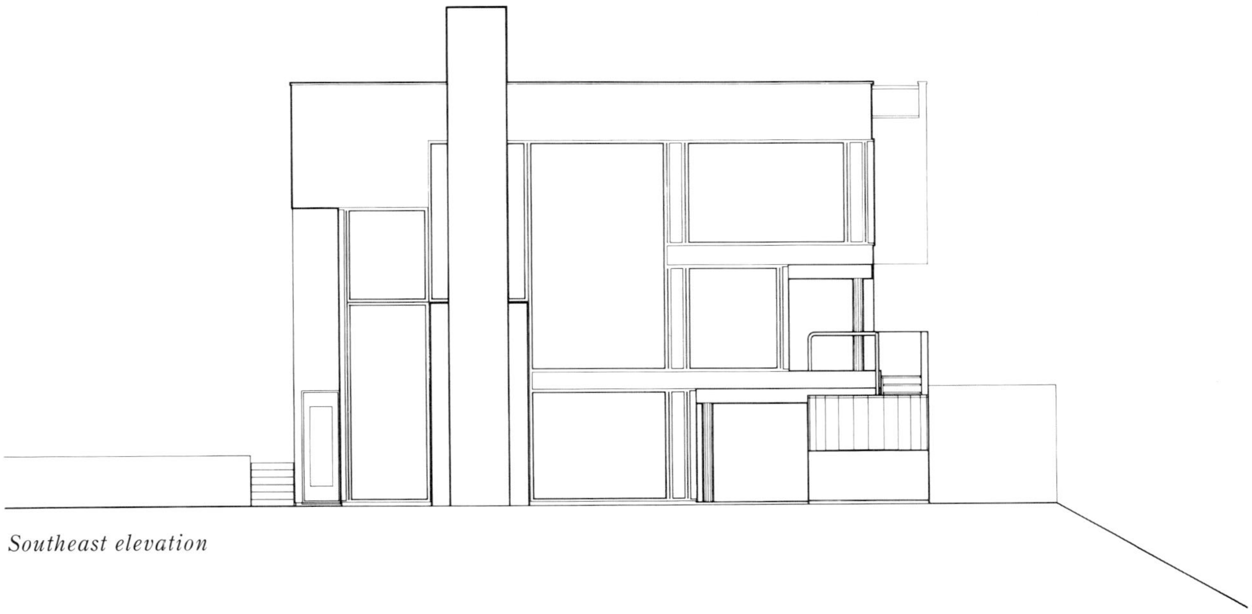

Southeast elevation

Southeast elevation

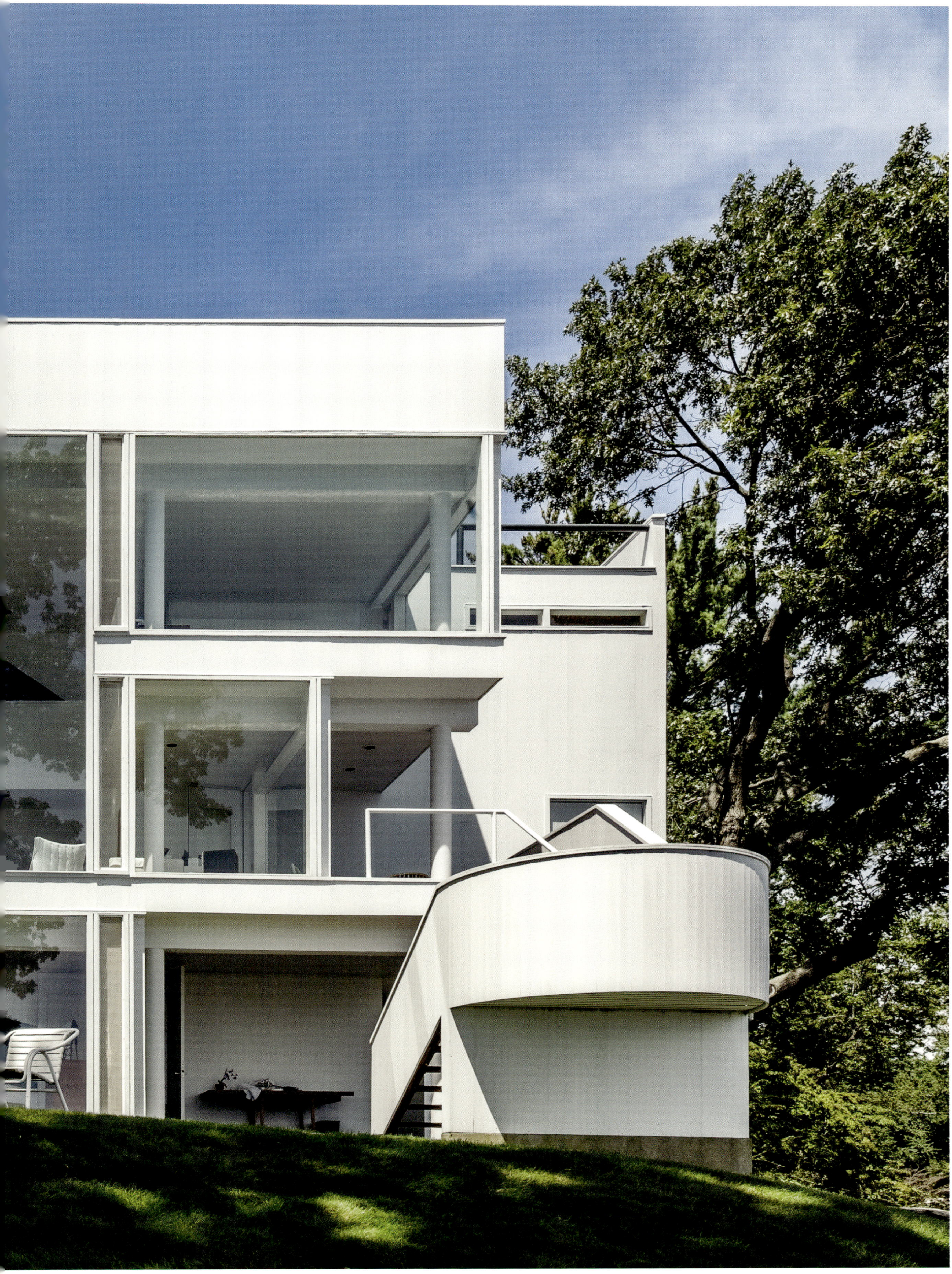

South corner: detail

Partial southeast elevation

Northwest elevation. View toward entrance

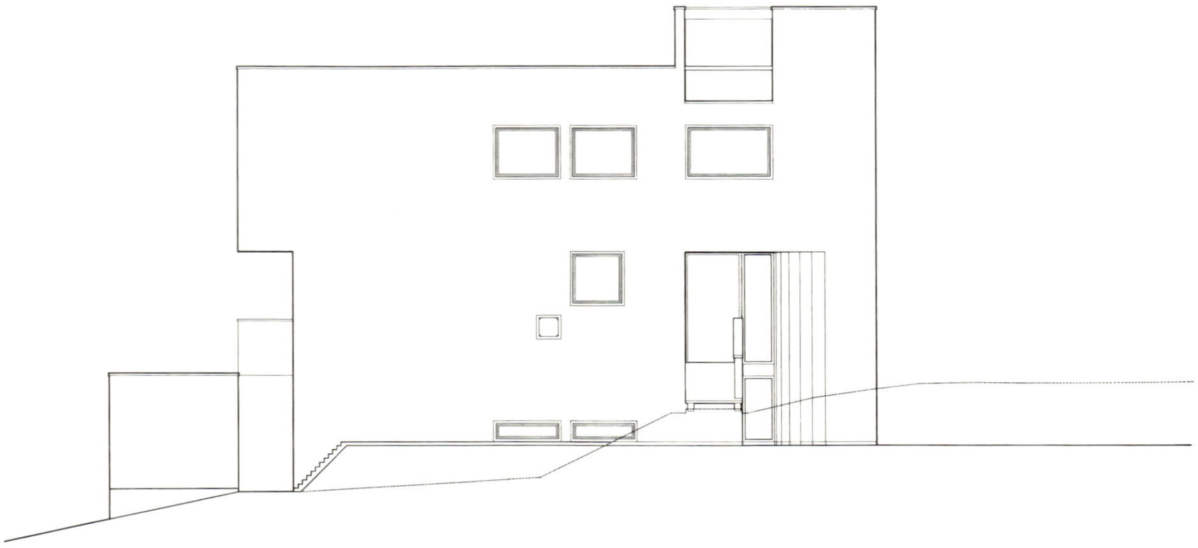

Northwest elevation

Southwest elevation

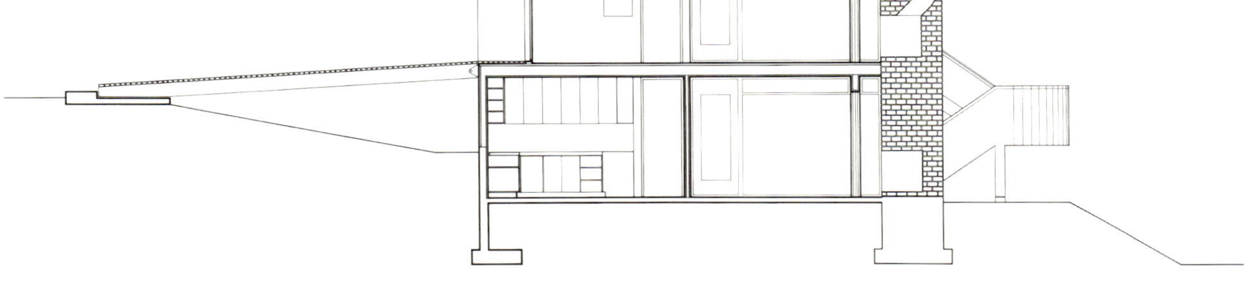

Cross section

Entrance

View from entrance toward living room

Living room: looking southeast

Living room: looking southwest

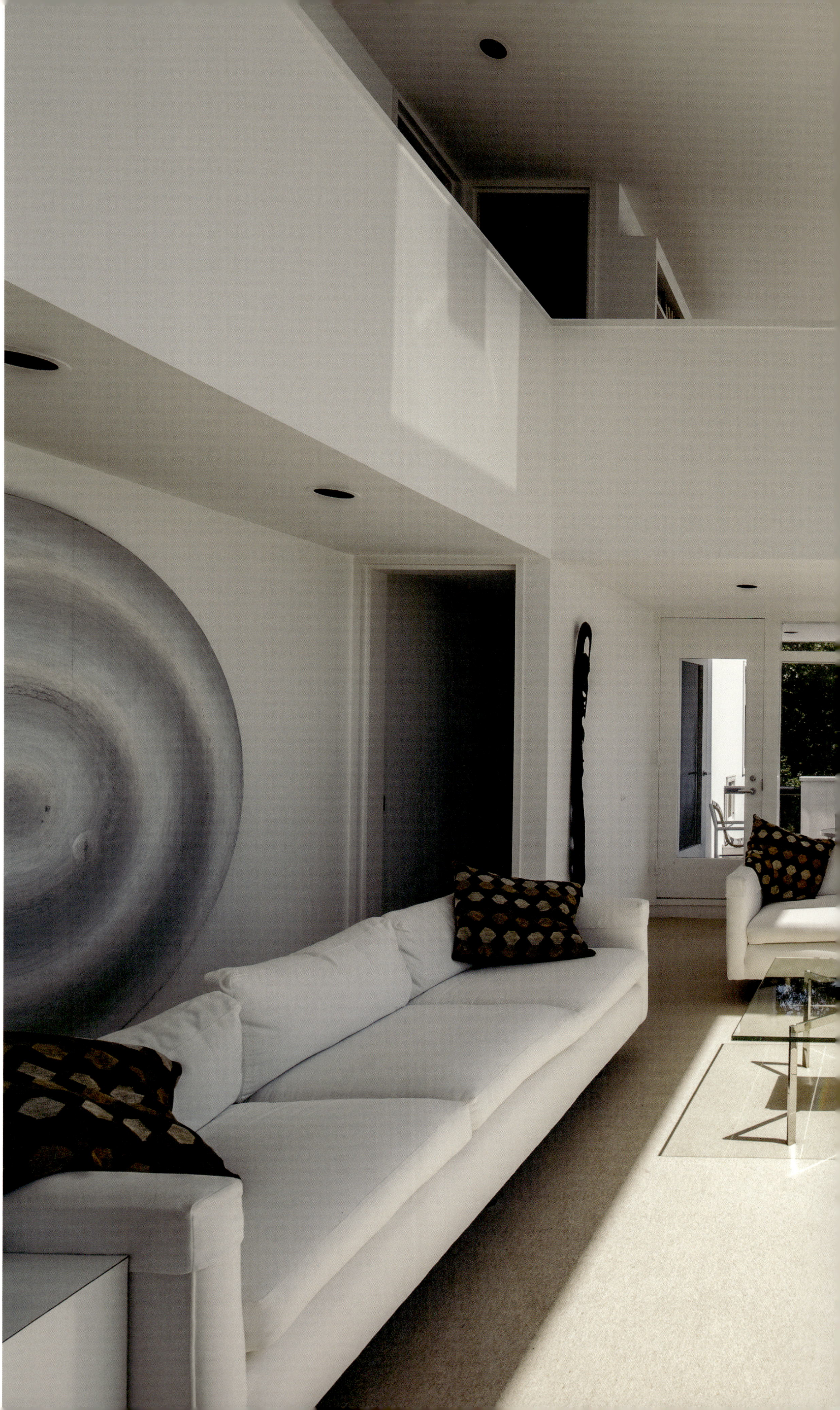

Living room

Corner of living room

View from veranda: column

Living room: view from upper level

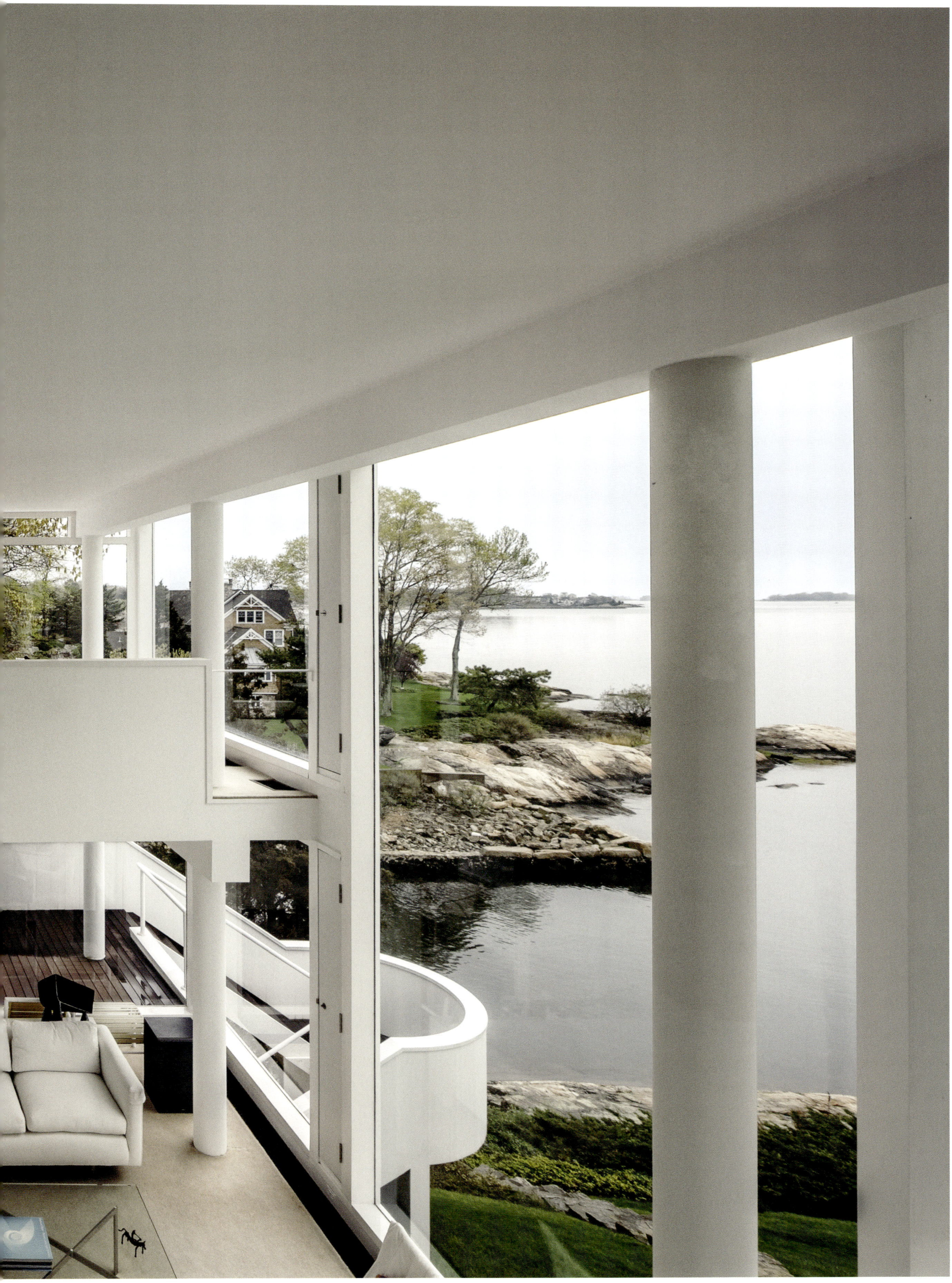

View toward garden on southwest through living room

Void on southwest: column at corner of dining room

Study on upper level

Dining room on lower level

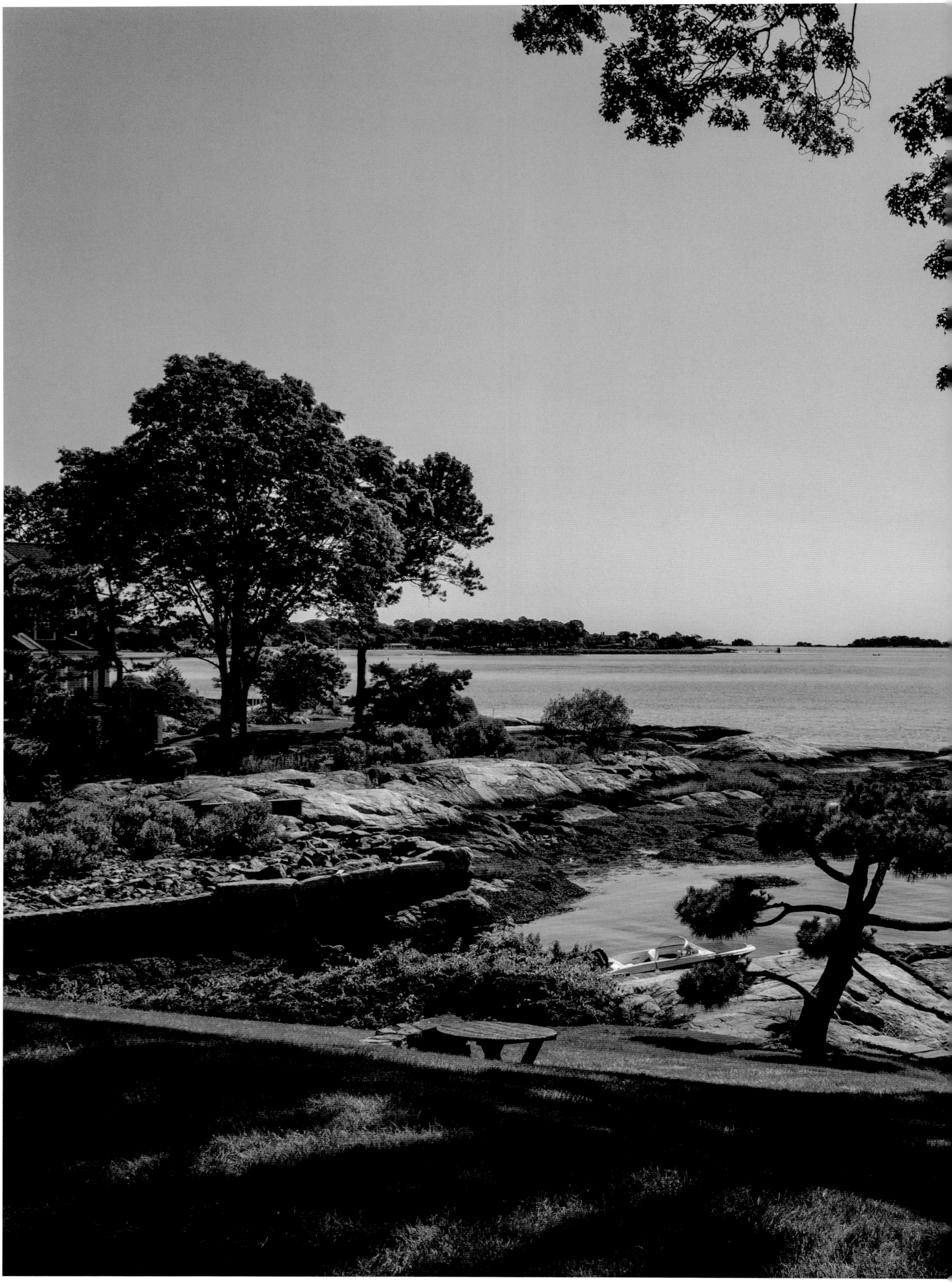

Panoramic view of Long Island Sound

View from Lake Michigan

Douglas House 1971-73

Upward view of west elevation

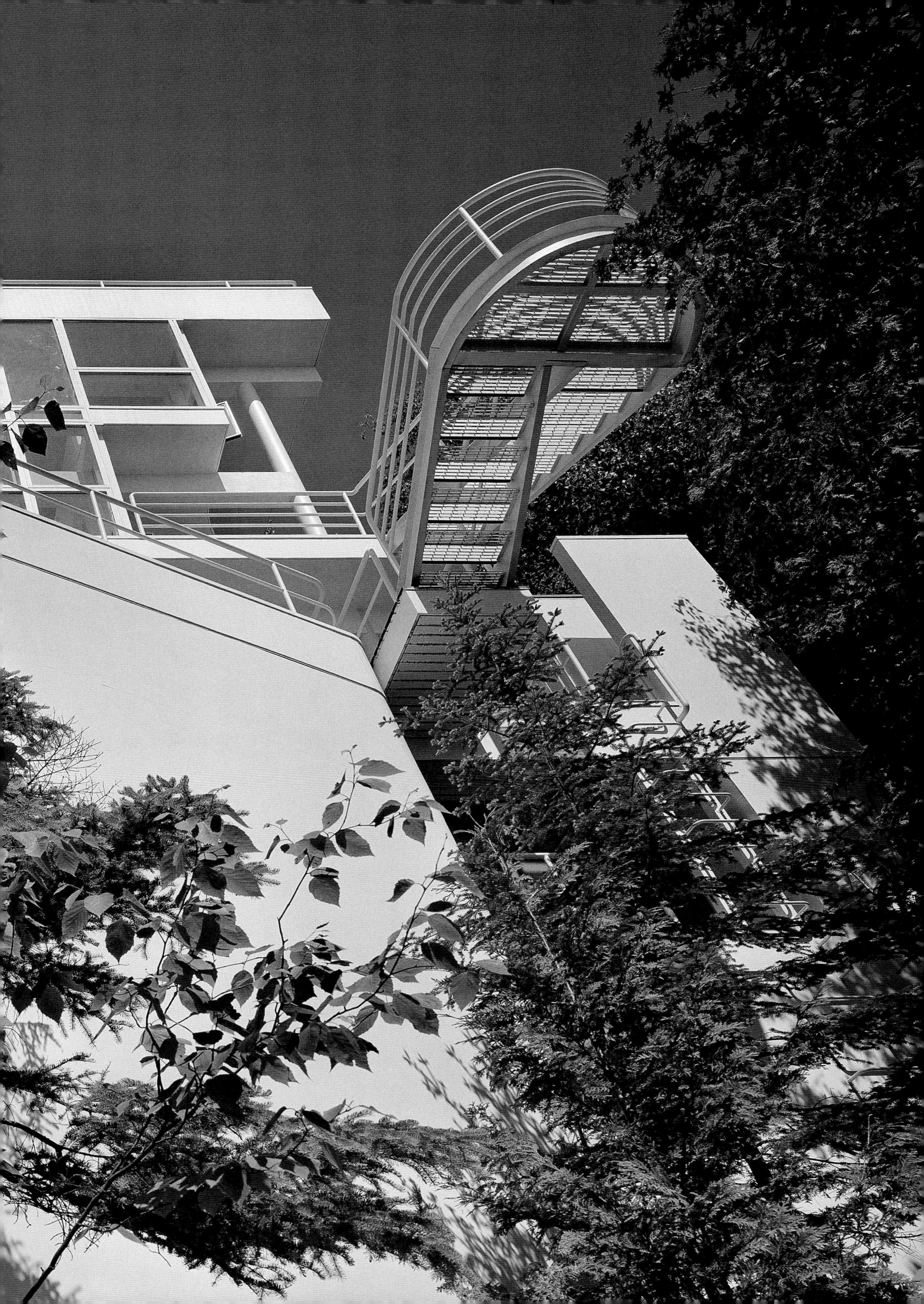

East elevation. Approach bridge to entrance.

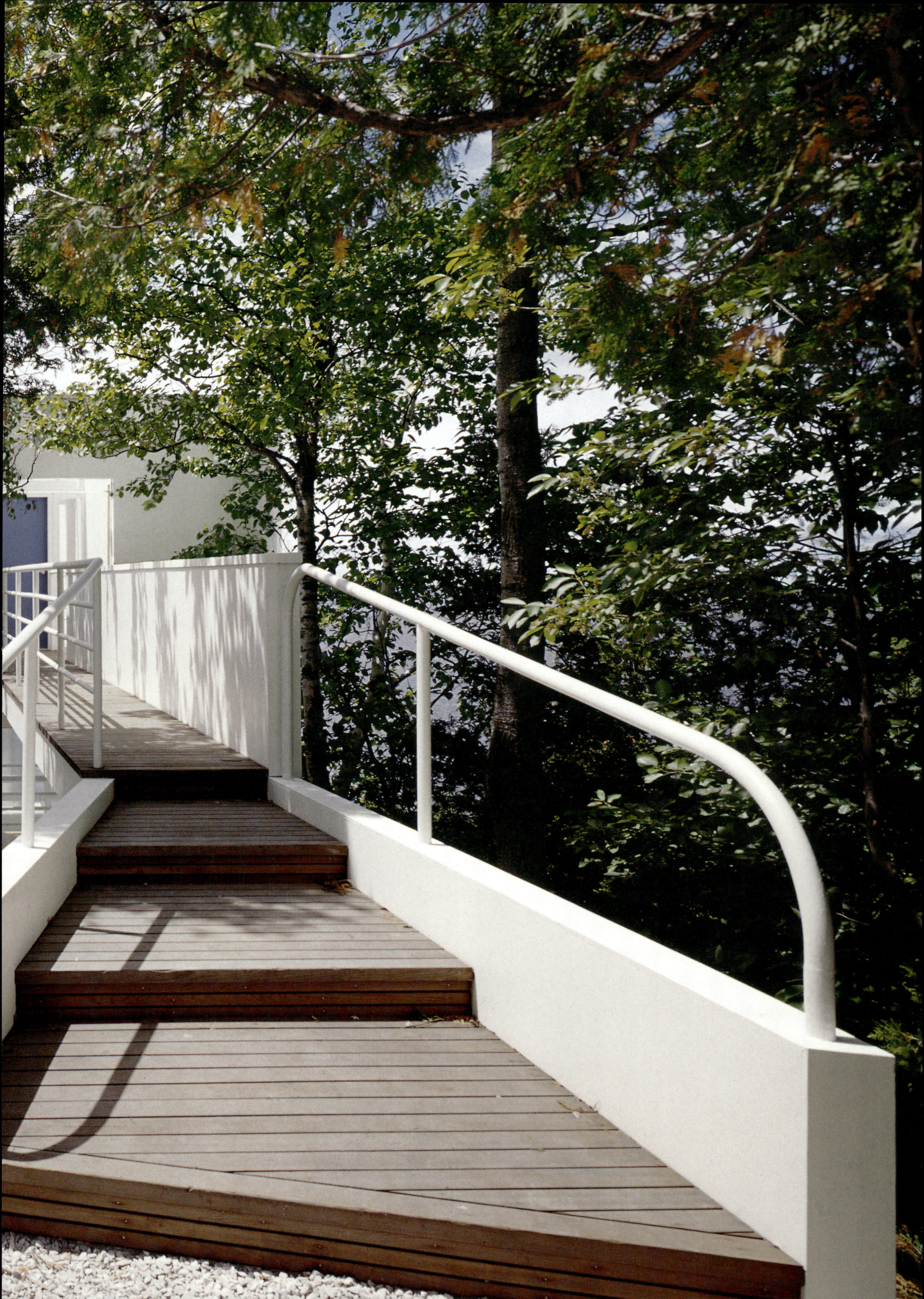

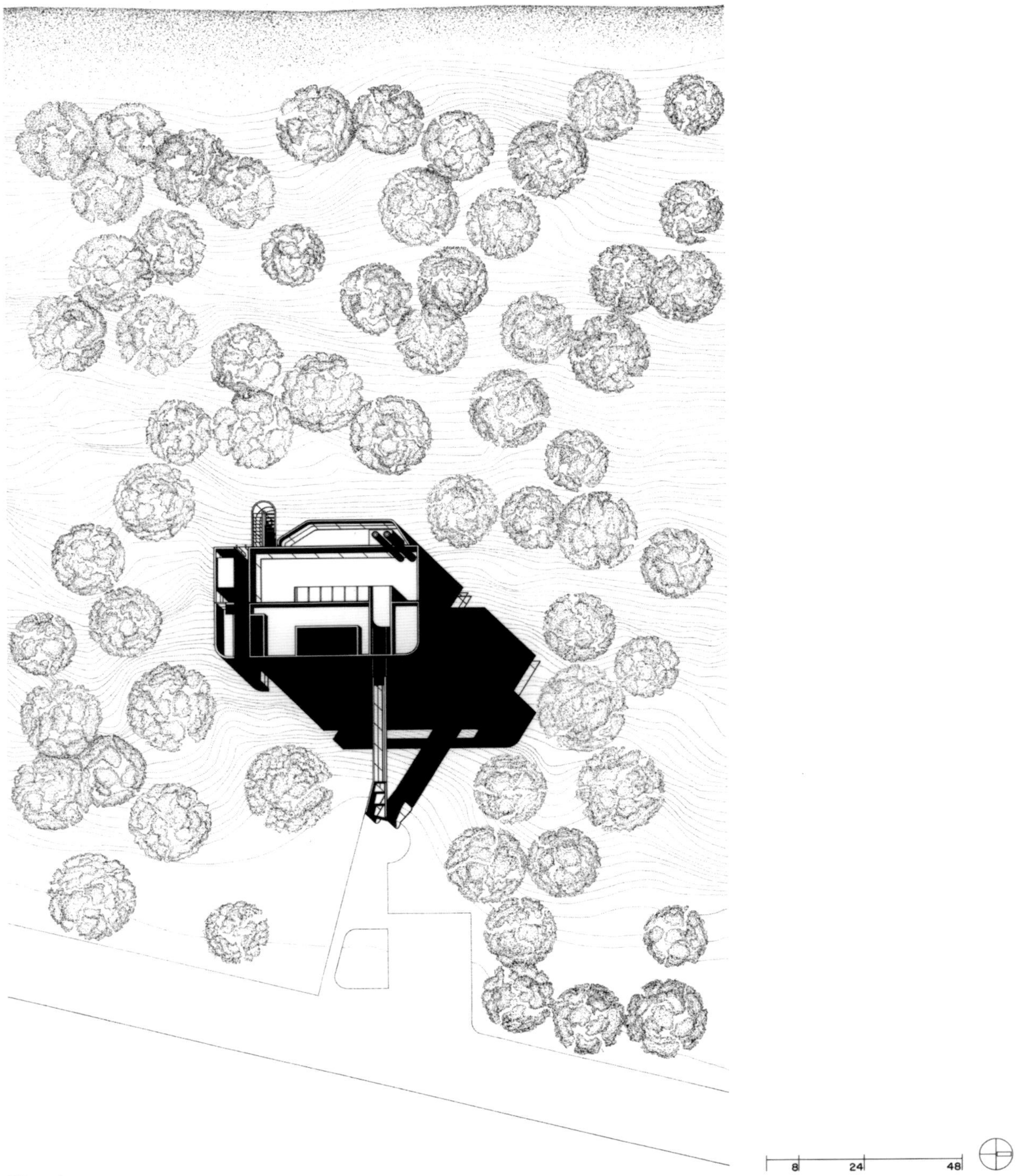

Site plan

South elevation

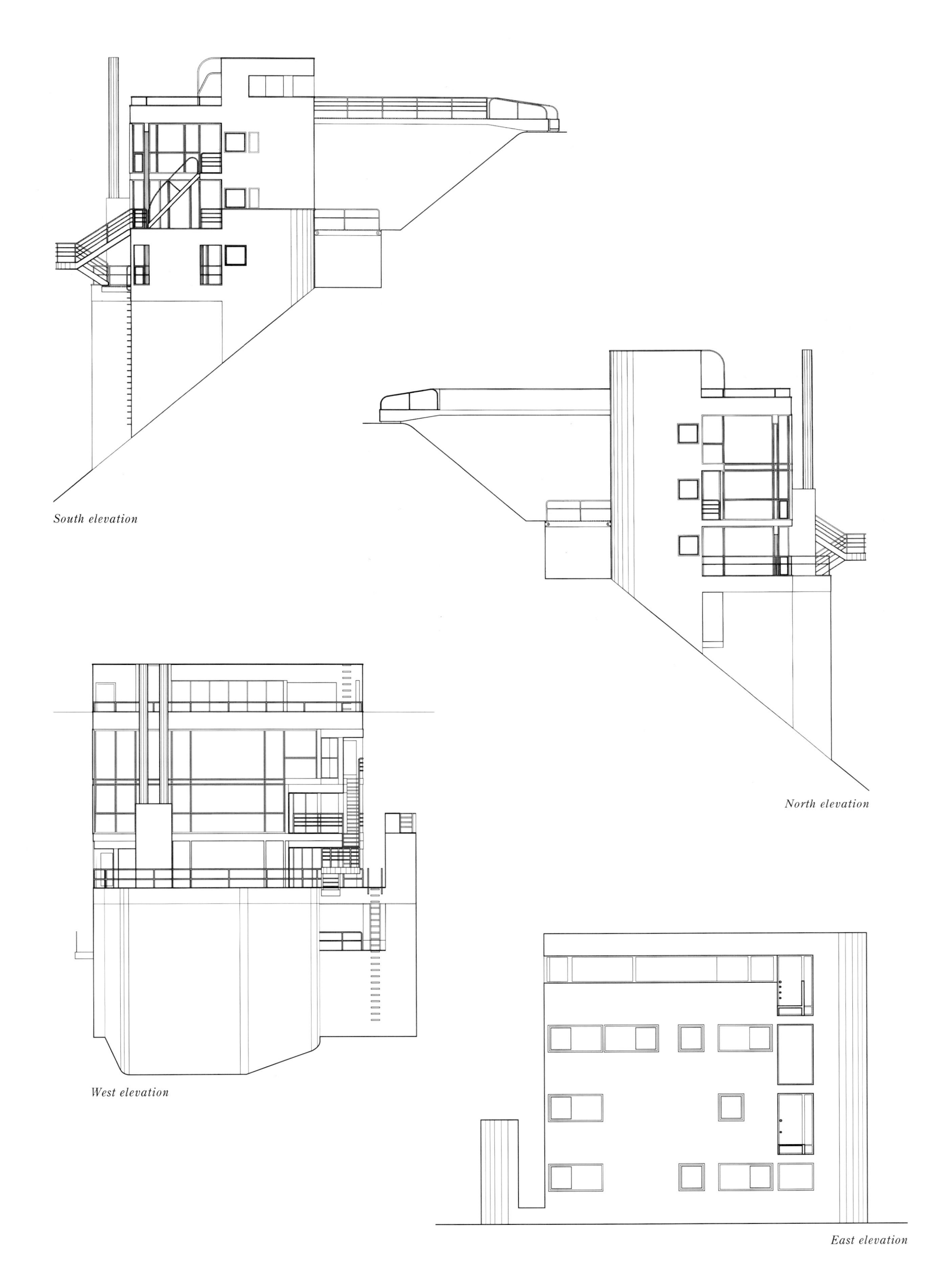

North elevation

West elevation

East elevation

Entrance

Deck on entrance level: view toward approach bridge

Deck on entrance level: looking west

49

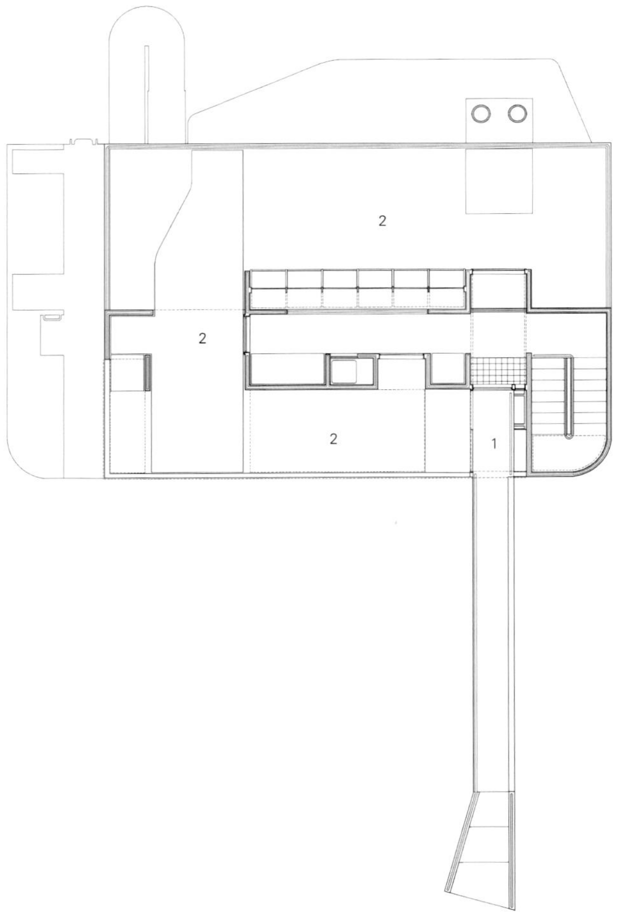

Entrance level

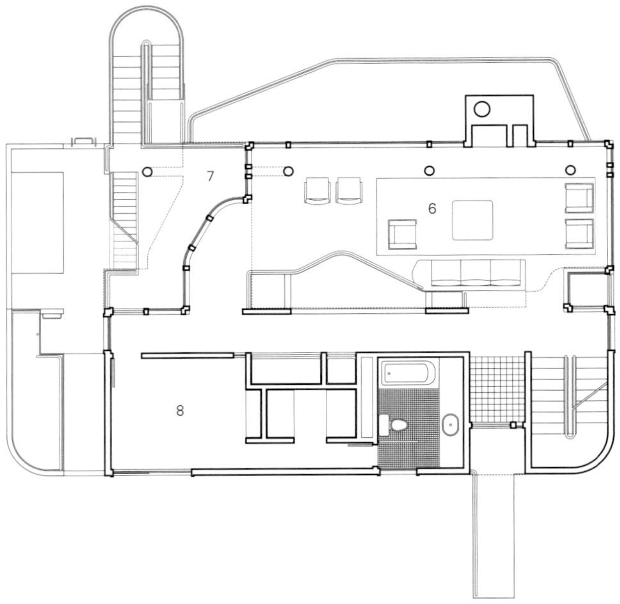

Middle level

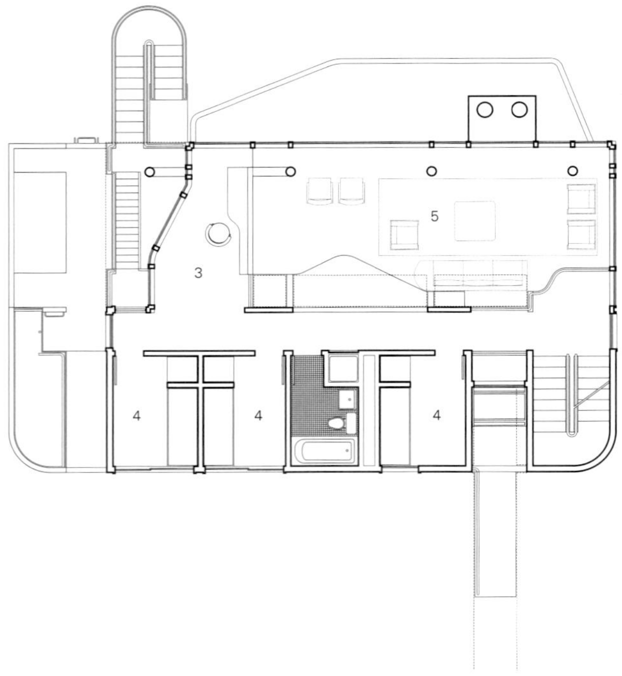

Upper level

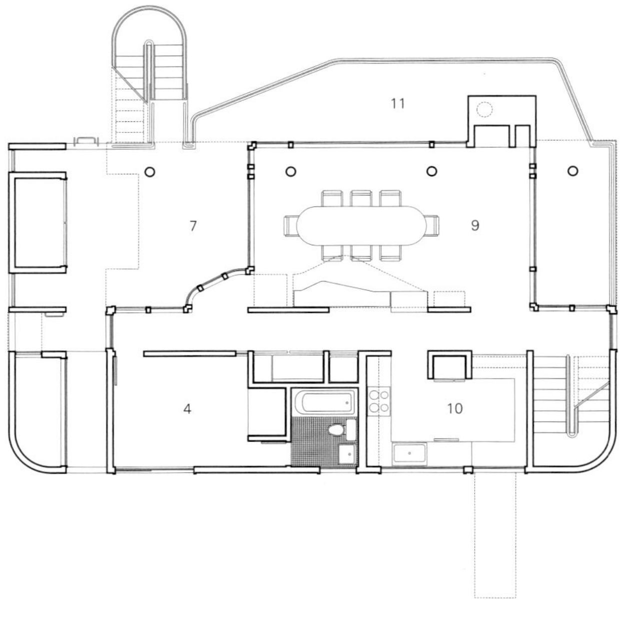

Lower level

1 ENTRANCE
2 DECK
3 STUDY
4 BEDROOM
5 VOID
6 LIVING ROOM
7 TERRACE
8 MASTER BEDROOM
9 DINING ROOM
10 KITCHEN
11 VERANDA

50

Cross section

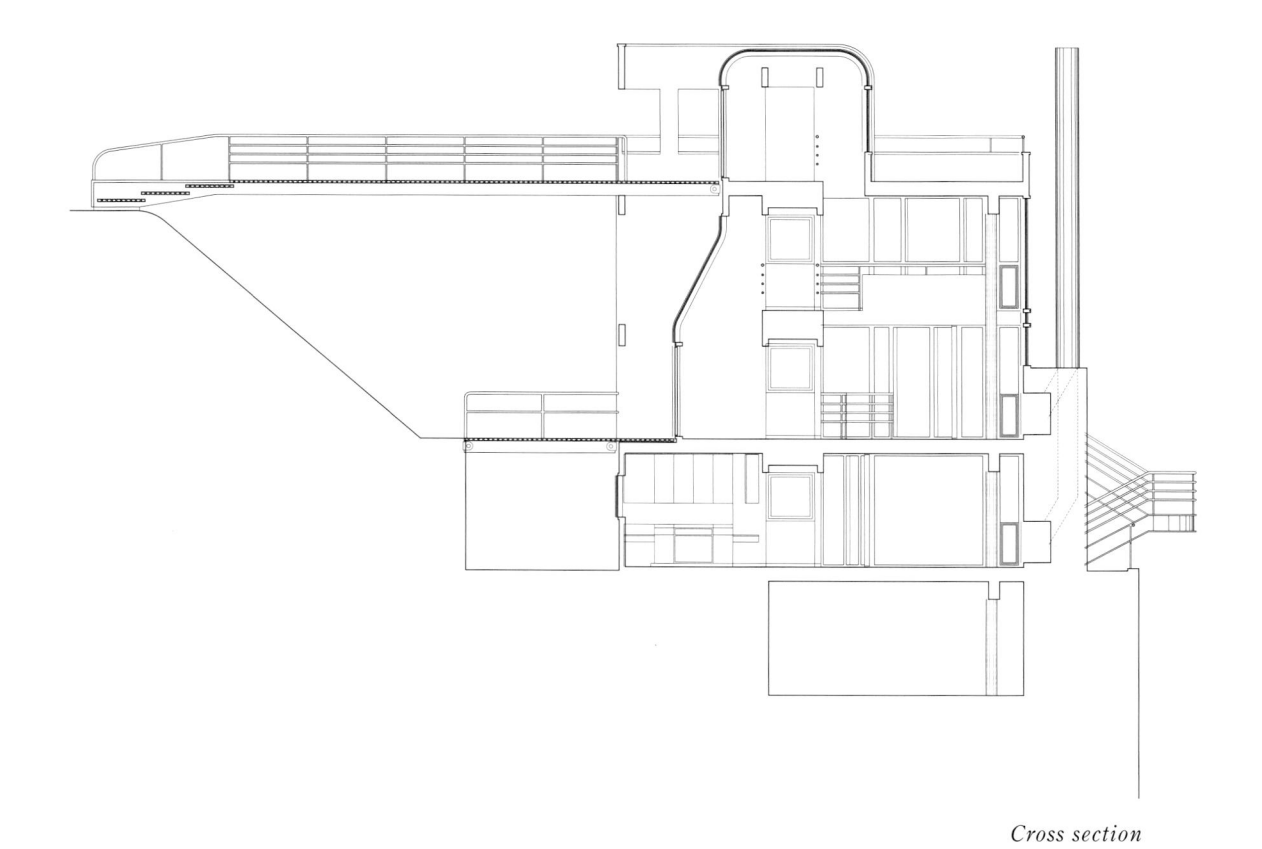

Longitudinal section

West deck facing on Lake Michigan

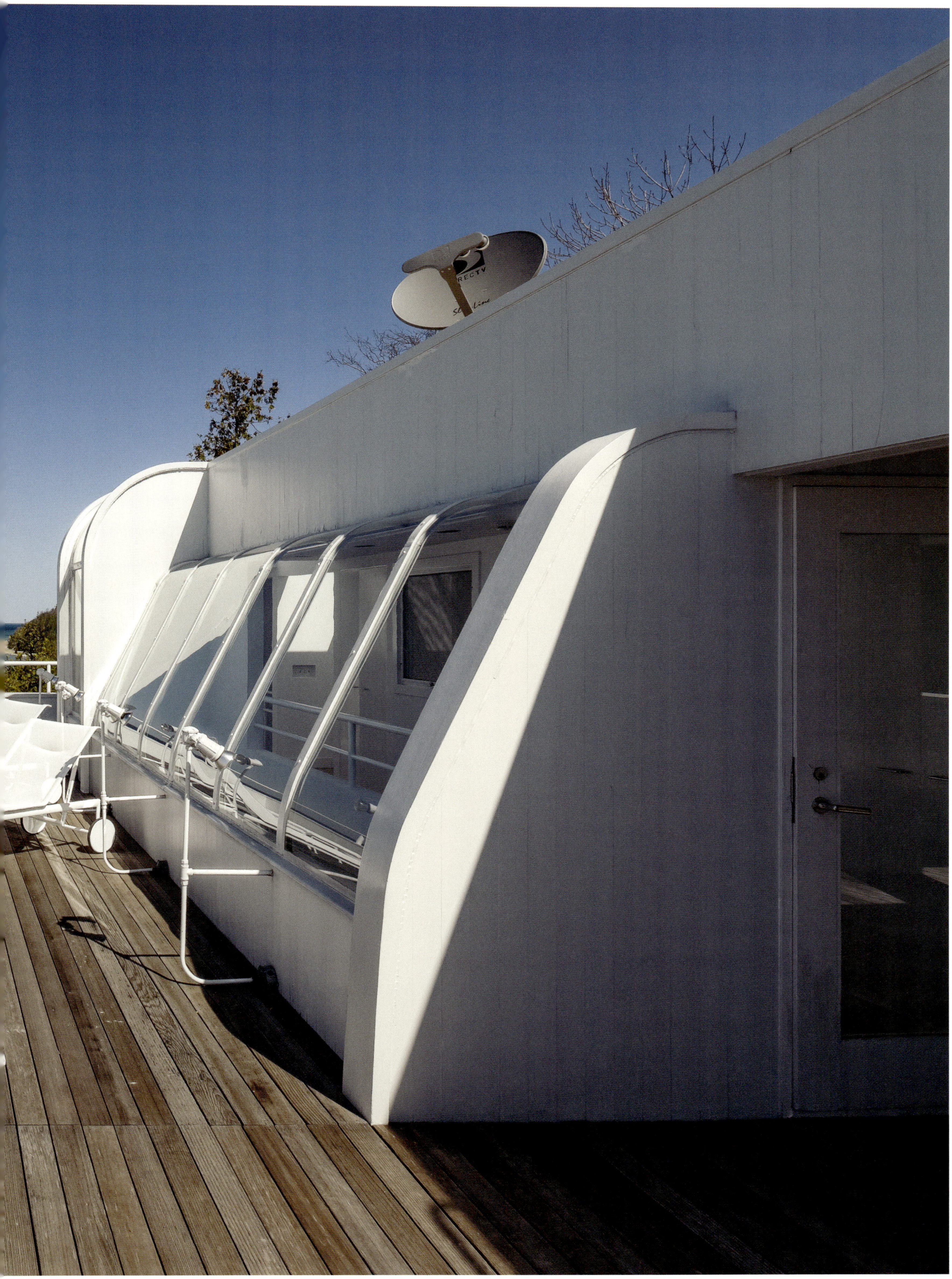

Hallway on entrance level. Deck on left

Upper level. Void of living room with skylight and north view

Downward view from entrance level toward living room and dining room

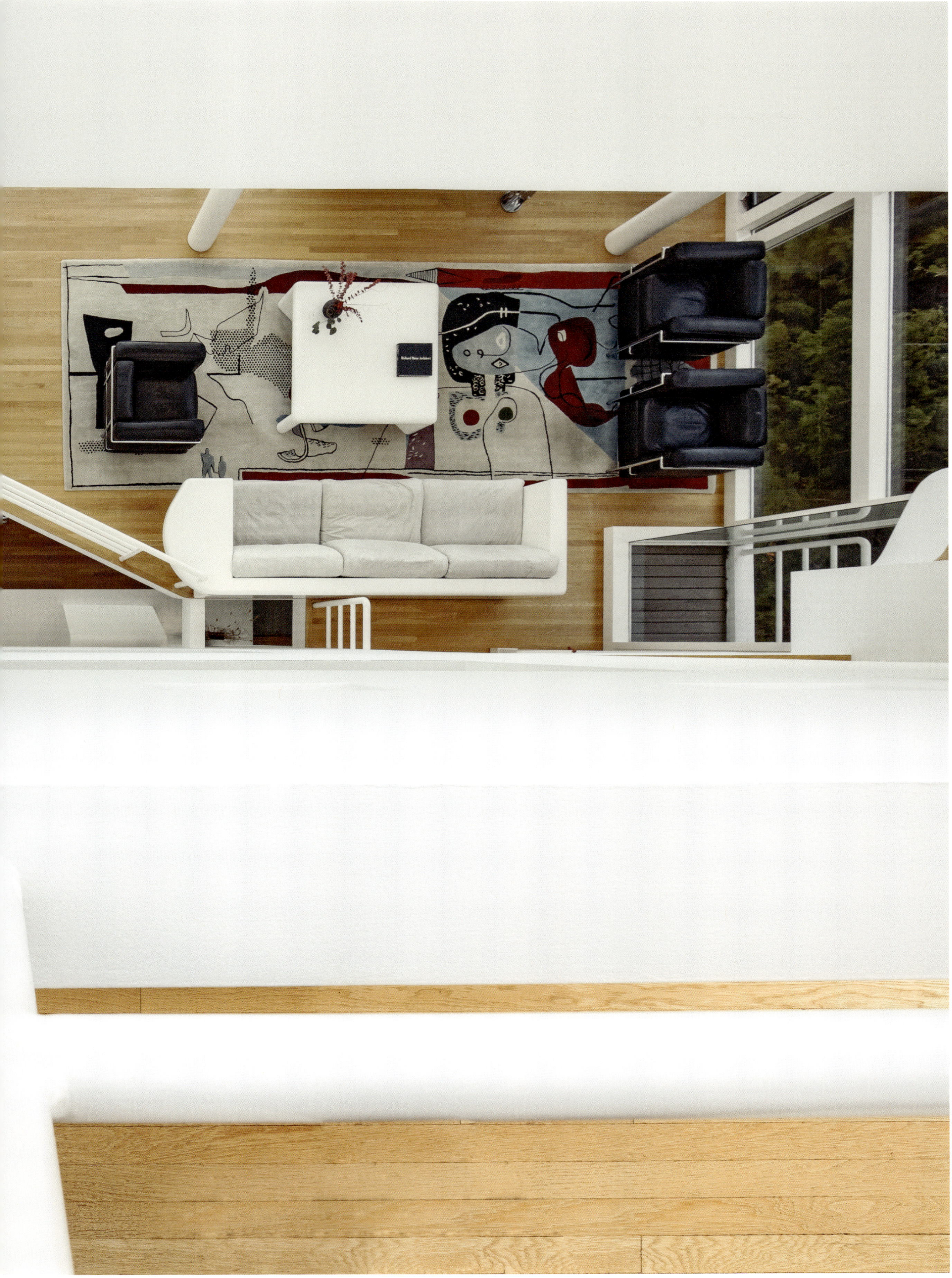

Upper level. View toward study. Living room below

Study

Living room: view from study on upper level

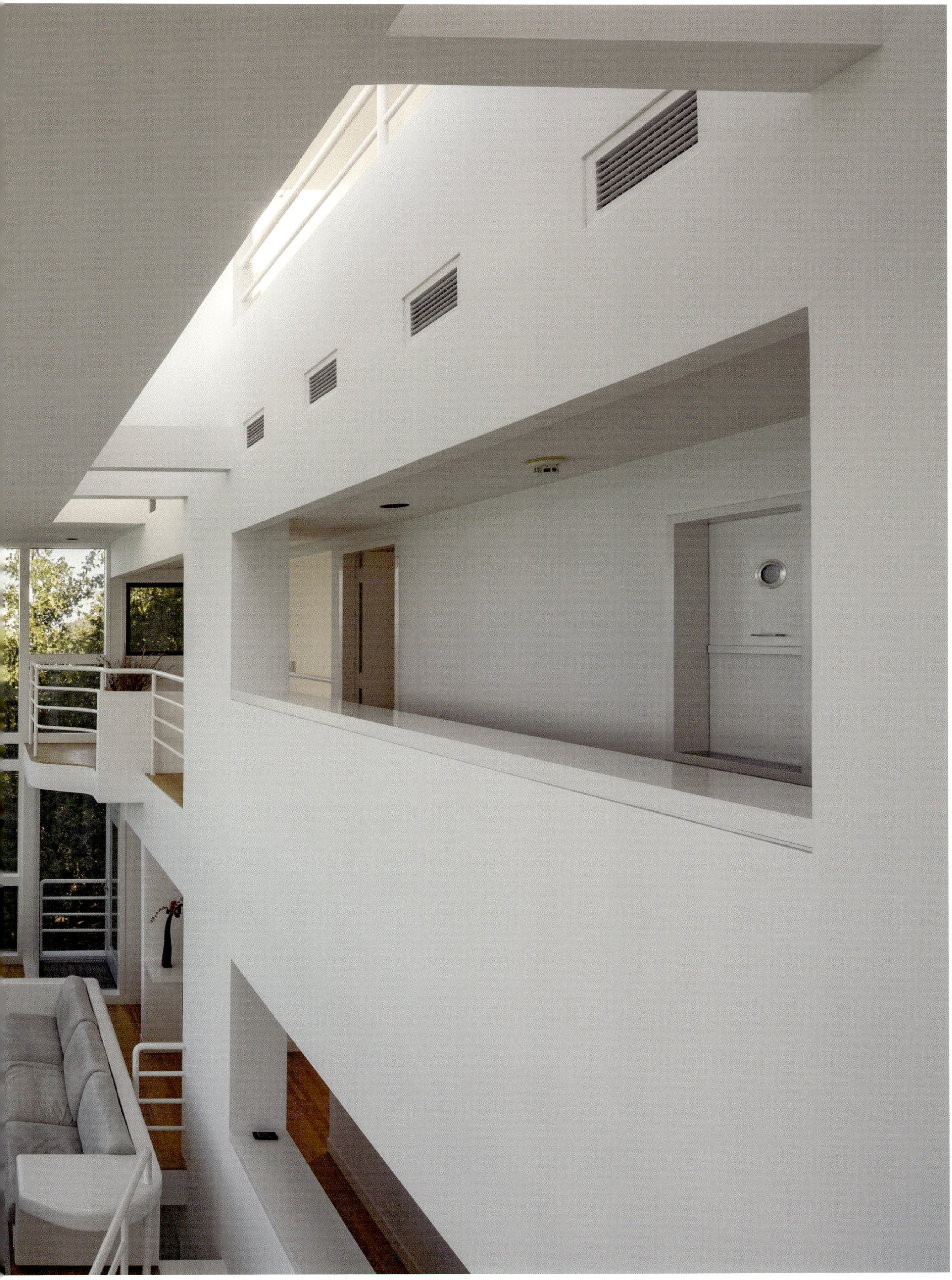

Living room

63

Living room. Looking north

Living room. Looking south

Corner of living room

Corner of living room: staircase and projected balcony

Dining room on lower level. Void connecting dining room and living room above

Dining room: view toward kitchen

Dining room

Dining room

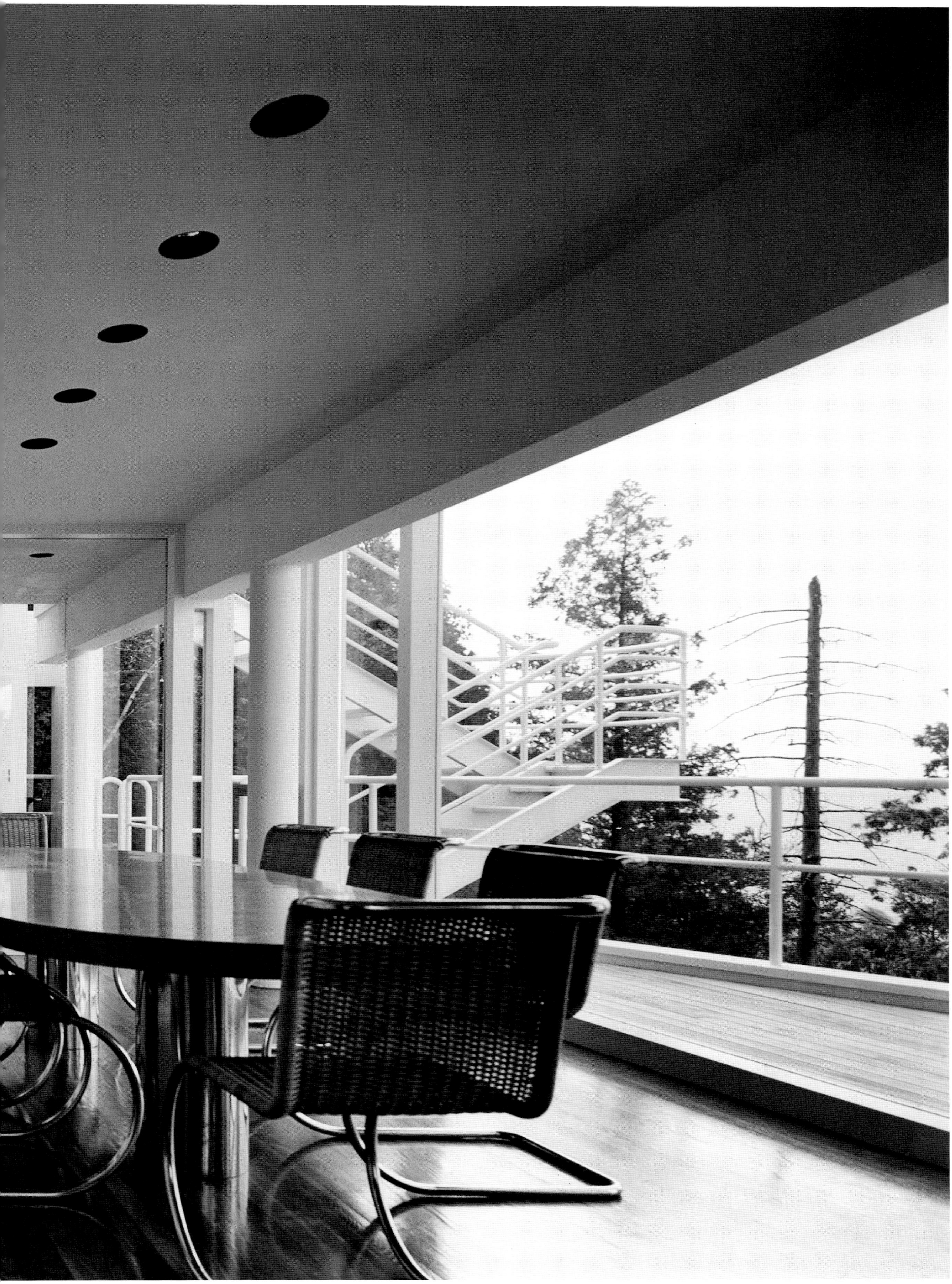

Terrace next to dining room on lower level

Hallway next to bedrooms on upper level

Bedroom on upper level

Master bedroom on middle level. View toward terrace

Master bedroom

View toward veranda on lower level

Veranda on lower level

Cantilevered stairway

Downward view of stairway

Deck on entrance level and Lake Michigan

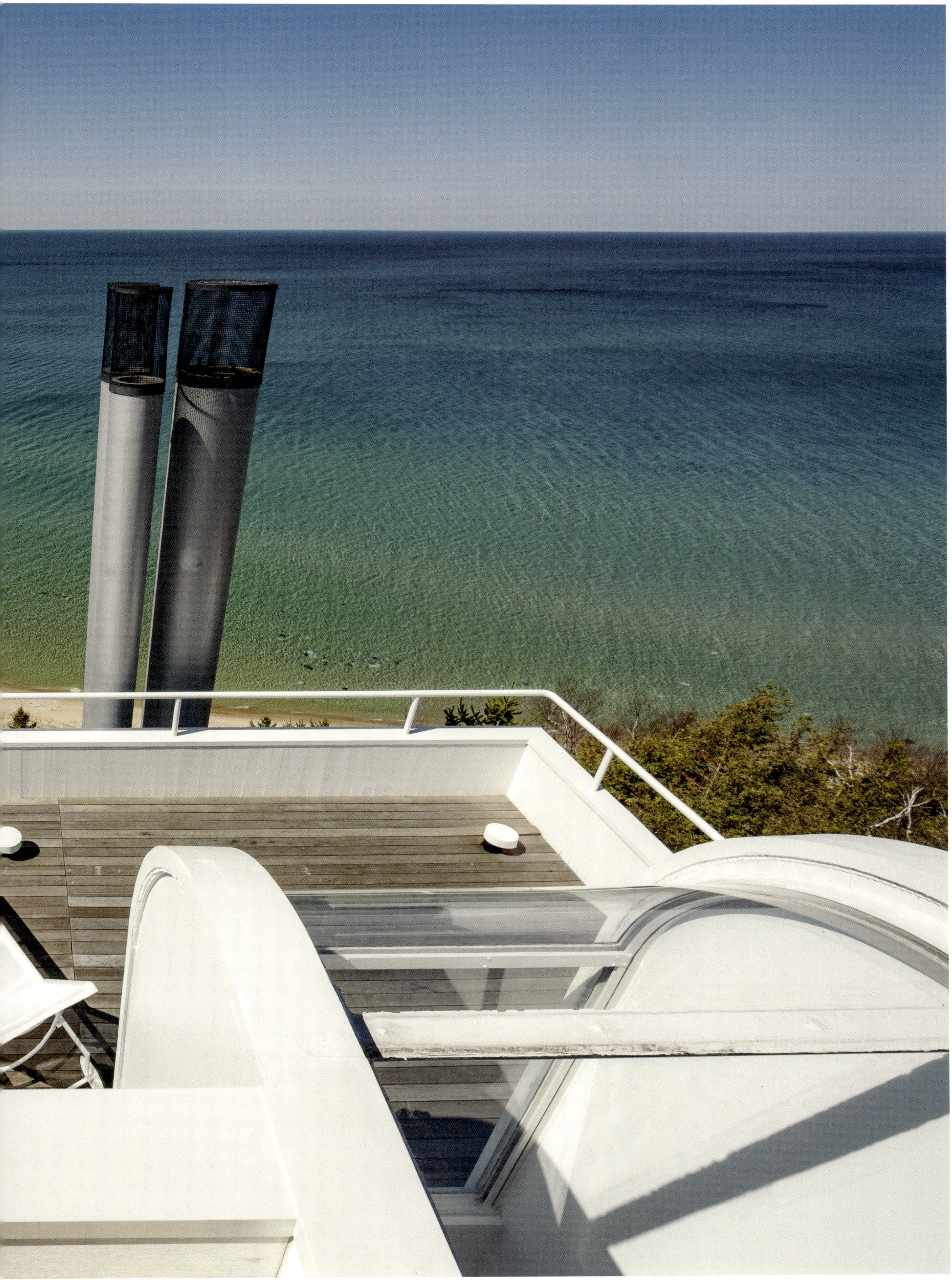

世界現代住宅全集17
リチャード・マイヤー
スミス邸
ダグラス邸

2014年11月25日発行
文・編集：二川由夫
撮影：二川幸夫
アート・ディレクション：細谷巖
印刷・製本：大日本印刷株式会社
制作・発行：エーディーエー・エディタ・トーキョー
151-0051　東京都渋谷区千駄ヶ谷3-12-14
TEL.(03)3403-1581(代)

禁無断転載
ISBN 978-4-87140-642-0 C1352